Bibliographic information published by the German National Library:

The German National Library lists this publication in the National Bibliography; detailed bibliographic data are available on the Internet at http://dnb.dnb.de .

Imprint:

Copyright © 2015 GRIN Verlag, Open Publishing GmbH
Print and binding: Books on Demand GmbH, Norderstedt Germany
ISBN: 9783668547650

This book at GRIN:

Http://www.grin.com/en/e-book/376574/what-leads-an-it-outsourcing-company-to-succeed

Amney Mounir

What leads an IT outsourcing company to succeed?

A Case Study. Helios Solutions and IT Outsourcing Company in India

GRIN Publishing

GRIN - Your knowledge has value

Since its foundation in 1998, GRIN has specialized in publishing academic texts by students, college teachers and other academics as e-book and printed book. The website www.grin.com is an ideal platform for presenting term papers, final papers, scientific essays, dissertations and specialist books.

Visit us on the internet:

Http://www.grin.com/

Http://www.facebook.com/grincom

Http://www.twitter.com/grin_com

Master Thesis

What leads an IT outsourcing company to succeed?

Case study : Helios Solutions, IT outsourcing company in India

ABSTRACT

This research paper is mainly focusing on the major factors that are behind a successful IT outsourcing business. It will be supported by an extensive literature review on the subject and by my own experience. It will also rely on the interviews I had and recommendations that I will put forward to remedy the challenges the company might face.

MOUNIR Amney
Master ICE (Innovation, Creation and Entrepreneurship)
EPF Enginnering School student
Academic year: 2016

Acknowledgments:

I would like to thank my family first for their support in carrying out this thesis. Their support was important, to say the least, and this work could not be accomplished without them.

I cannot deny the fact that I have lived the greatest experience of my life so far. For that, I would like to thank India for making this possible.

Special thanks go to my tutor Anne-Soto Mayor who provided with a valuable assistance to fulfill my thesis.

Table of Contents

I. Introduction

Nowadays, the world of business is becoming more and more competitive. For this reason, many companies are tempted to differentiate themselves from other firms by optimizing their cost and making more profits. To achieve this objective, they resort to what is generally referred to as outsourcing. In fact, they delegate some of their business to an external party in order to be more focused on their own core competencies.

It is true that outsourcing is a global phenomenon that deals with many trade areas such as industry and information technology (IT), which remains definitely the leading field up to 64% of the outsourcing market size worldwide [1].

Despite the popularity of this phenomenon, outsourcing companies throughout the world find it harder and harder to maintain their existing customers. So far no clear answers have been raised as to the success or failure of an IT outsourcing project. The experience I have had in India, renowned country in this field, pushed me to reflect on this issue and raise many questions.

a. Problem statement and research questions

For a better understanding of the issue stated above, let me go over my experience at Helios Solutions, an IT outsourcing company in India. This firm offers many services in subtracting such as mobile and software development, creation of websites and Internet marketing and it is exclusively devoted to the European market. Within the company, my job consisted mainly of managing and coordinating projects with the French market (France and Switzerland). Practically speaking, I had to make sure that Helios Solutions customers' requirements are well understood. Here I acted mainly as a go between the clients and the developers to see that the

---

[1] Science and Technology for Development: the New Paradigm of ICT, 2007, p.123

message got through. As a project manager, my role consisted in supervising the developers throughout the whole project. I also had to solve bugs and other matters related to the customers' feedbacks along with the development team related to Helios Solutions' services.

During my training in Helios Solutions, I learned how to communicate effectively with developers, having meetings on a regular basis and assume considerable responsibilities. All these acquirements helped me to learn and self-develop with time. Indeed, thanks to this experience I learned to manage a team more efficiently, and go a lot of technical know-how like leadership, decision-making, problem solving and initiative taking. Faced with some challenges and limitations during my training related to cross-cultural differences, I raised the following questions:

- How do European customers conceive outsourcing? Do they really account for differences related to culture, the language being used in communication and interpersonal interaction?
- How to handle internal communication with a totally different culture?
- How can we bridge the cultural and communication gap between the different intervenants in the outsourcing process?

b. Research objective

The questions that I raised above were behind the background and layout of my research paper. This had led me to reflect on what makes a successful and efficient IT outsourcing projects in a cross-cultural environment.

c. Scope and limitations

To answer the problematic dealt above, I will rely on the theoretical background based on an extensive literature review and on my own practical experience in an IT outsourcing company. This latter will be supported by all the interviews I had and the recommendations that I will put forward to remedy the challenges the case company might face.

d. Thesis structure

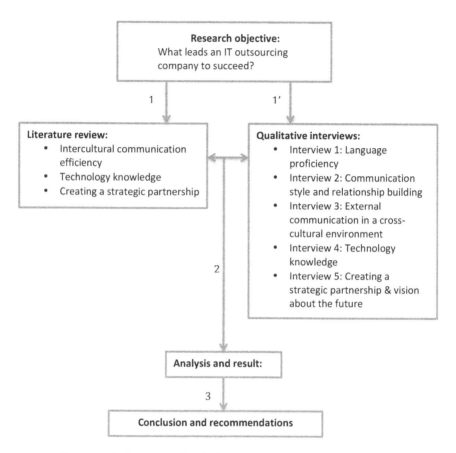

Figure 1.4: Thesis structure of my thesis

II. Sustainable development and corporate social responsibility

Before moving to the theoretical framework of my research paper, I am required to comply with the "Green Plan for Higher Education establishment" that states

"Sustainable development and corporate social responsibility" as an area mandatory to cover.

As a first step, we will define what *sustainable development and corporate social responsibility* is. Understanding this concept is mandatory to apply it in a realistic case. To achieve this, we will assess its three main dimensions, (environmental, social and economical aspects) by taking Helios Solutions as case of study. To conclude, I will give recommendations to this latter in this field.

a. Definition

This concept, that takes too long to write, consists in taking into consideration social and environmental impact of company's activities in order to meet the challenges of sustainable development. The objective of this concept is to join together its economical, social and environment aspects in an ethical way.

b. Assessment of the three main dimensions of this concept

As we have already stated, the three main dimensions of this concept are:

- Environmental dimension
- Social dimension
- Economical dimension

As we all know India and environment are not the best friends. Helios Solutions is unfortunately no exception to the rule. The only things that have been set-up within the company to preserve the environment are:

- Use of LED light to reduce electricity consumption
- An energy-efficient flush tank in order to reduce water consumption

These are the only things that have been implemented in the environmental aspect.

However, many actions have been taken to ensure a decent social cohesion at Helios Solutions, which are:

- Decent salary and health insurance
- No differentiation in terms of salary and rights between man and woman

- Pleasant working condition
- International environment: many people from different nationalities are working within the company.

In addition, for the economical aspect, Helios Solutions allocate every year a budget for its employees' leisure purpose. They actually plan on a regular basis a trip that also helps for a better cohesion in the group.

c. Recommendations for Helios Solutions

These are the recommendations I would like to give for each dimension of corporate social responsibility of Helios Solutions:

- Environment recommendations:
  - They have to recycle their daily waste by giving it to recycling companies instead of throwing it away.
  - Use recycled paper
  - Use a presence sensor for electricity
  - Use of solar energy with photovoltaic panels

These environmental recommendations might not be in the company's scope, as the city itself does not have enough facilities in order to make all of this possible.

- Social recommendations:
  - Disabled facilities
  - Find ways to motivate the team (employee of the month, get prices)
  - Get a regular feedback from employees in order to make eventual changes within the company
- Economical recommendations
  - Allocate a part of the budget for associations

After having reviewed all the recommendations that should be taken by Helios Solutions in a future basis, we will now consider the next chapter of my research paper: the theoretical base.

III.   Theoretical base

Based on an extensive literature review, this chapter is outlining the reasons behind a successful IT outsourcing project. Recent documents, books and articles have supported this framework. This section consists in understanding outsourcing and information technology outsourcing in particular and explaining the reasons India is considered as a hub for these services in Europe. However the main concern of this theoretical study is to understand what impact intercultural communication, strategic partnership and technology knowledge have on leading an IT outsourcing project to success.

a.   Definition of outsourcing

1.   General view of outsourcing

To be more profitable and get a smile from shareholders, European companies have a tendency to outsource their services. This all started in the 1950s (Dibbern et al., 2004; Quinn and Hilmer, 1994) and became a viable strategy a few years after. Despite its fame, this phenomenon is not understood by all and often leads to misunderstandings. So, what is outsourcing?

Outsourcing is the fact of giving a task or a service, which was performed internally to a third party. However, still a lot of people make confusions between outsourcing and offshoring. While offshoring is getting work done in a different country, outsourcing refers to contracting a job or a task to an external company or organization. Indeed, the word offshore outsourcing is commonly used to refer to outsourcing a service in a different country, and onshore outsourcing within the same country[2].

As a matter of fact, offshore outsourcing has been rising strongly since the 1950s. According to the Everest Research Institute, the worldwide outsourcing market size in 2005 was $362 billion of which IT outsourcing accounted for $233

---

[2] Vincent Jacques, International outsourcing strategy and competitiveness, 2006, p.19

9

billion (64 per cent) [3] and will keep growing at an annual rate of 7.7% [4]. Under those circumstances, speaking of outsourcing with no reference to its main field would be meaningless.

2. IT outsourcing

As mentioned before, information technology remains the largest industry sector for offshore outsourcing. Mahnke (2001) gives an explanation to this phenomenon as he considers that there is a growing pressure on management to remain efficient and effective by accomplishing more with fewer resources at a faster pace. In reality definition of IT outsourcing is much too wide and hard to process. Grover, Cheon and Teng (1996) made it clearer and more intelligible as they simply divide IT outsourcing into application development and maintenance, system operation, networks/telecommunication management, end-user computing support, system planning and management, and application software purchase. [5]

Of course, IT outsourcing is evolving year in and year out but buyers or suppliers has always to deal with risks in their projects[6] according to Ian Tho (2005). So what are the risks related to outsourcing an IT project?

3. Risks

In the IT outsourcing industry, a lot of risks may come to the surface such as service quality as it is considered by Ian Tho (2005) like "a major issue". Indeed, it is not possible to deny the fact that outsourcing a service to a third part can sometimes lead to bad surprises. According to a survey made by Deloitte in 2012 targeting 157 private and public sector organizations (that are outsourcing a part of their business activities) only 62% were satisfied with the service provided and 32% were likely neutral. Considering outsourcing like a way to save costs and time, this risk can result

---

[3] Science and Technology for Development: the New Paradigm of ICT, 2007, p.123
[4] John K. Halvey, Barbara Murphy, Information Technology Outsourcing Transactions, 2005, p.3
[5] Volker Mhanke, Mikel Overby, Jan Vang, Strategic IT outsourcing: "What do we know and need to know?" 2003, p.4
[6] Ian Tho, Managing the risks of IT outsourcing, 2005, p.15

in having the opposite of the intended effect. This could lead the company, which is outsourcing to either stop delegating their services or find a new service provider.

Here comes a risk of finding or choosing the right service provider as according to Robert J. Trent and Llewellyn R. Roberts (2009) is "the key to a successful outsourcing experience" [7]. Unfortunately, this risk is significant as the search area is global and distance does not help. For Robert J. Trent (2009), "distance is the main barrier" for choosing the right service provider, as it is more often located really far and makes the possibility to visit and then evaluate really hard.

In addition to that, miscommunication can result from the language being used, or by a complete misunderstanding of the requirements. Kevin T. McDonald (2010) emphasizes the fact that service quality staff plays a big role to avoid these misunderstandings as he mentions that an organization needs to have "the best program or project manager" otherwise "the risk that the resulting process is not understood is greater". [8] This miscommunication risk is a result of choosing the right service provider; this is to say a qualified staff.

In the same fashion, cultural differences are considered by many companies as a risk to fail an outsourcing project. According to Charles M. Vance and Yongsun Pai (2015) many "cross-cultural risk factors" could impact the success of an offshore outsourcing project. They point out the "differences in national cultures" which might affect not only business relationship but "also processes and work interactions". Another point mentioned is the possible misunderstanding of "nuances in communication style and language expression". This shows how working with a different culture might influence the outcome of an IT outsourcing project.

These are the most important risk factors that could lead companies to fail in the outsourcing experience according to the scope of this research. In the

---

[7] Robert J. Trent, Llewellyn R. Roberts, Managing Global Supply and Risk: Best Practices, Concepts, and Strategies, 2009, p. 98

[8] Kevin T. McDonald, Above the Clouds: Managing Risk in the World of Cloud Computing, 2010, p. 85

meantime, despite these risks IT outsourcing is not disturbed by these background noises. After all, what is the top country the companies have chosen to outsource to? According to a survey made by a consulting firm A.T Kearney (2014), India is the country which is considered as "unrivaled in both scale and people skills", particularly in the IT sector.

Concerning this popularity, a question comes up: What are the factors that make India an IT outsourcing magnet?

b. Why India is an IT outsourcing magnet?

1. An important workforce availability

Despite being one of the largest IT outsourcing destination, if not the world's largest as it holds the "biggest market's share" [9] India has an important workforce availability. In 2013, Nasscom (trade association of Indian IT and business outsourcing) gave an analysis of talent supply in the Indian IT industry. The figure shown below demonstrates how important the Indian talent pool is as the number of graduates has been rising every year since 2011. In 2013, India counted 0.77 millions graduates in the technical field among 5.01 millions graduates. Forecast has shown that this impressive improvement will be still on by 2020 with a tremendous number of 8.14 millions graduates. The important thing to point out is that the number of graduates in the IT field is growing much faster than the other sectors with an increase from 2013 to 2020 of 100%.

---

[9] Graham Earnshaw, China Business Guide, 2006, p.322

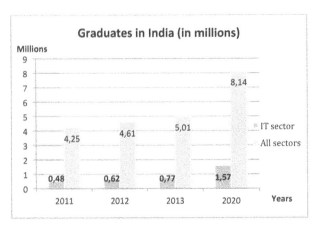

Figure 3.2.1: Number of graduates in Indian (Nasscom, TechSci Research)

This tremendous progress made India "the largest talent pool in the world"[10] but a further advantage is its low labour cost. According to a survey made by Oecd economics "India's greatest competitive advantage is in labour costs"[11].

2. Cost-cutting

Because of its growing economy and youth talent pool India is the new Eldorado for IT outsourcing. European companies are actually looking for this type of profile as according to Robert J. Trent and Llewellyn R. Roberts (2010) they look for these "in-between"[12] countries to "take advantage of lower-cost goods and services". By "in-between" the authors meant a country, which is between a third world country (low cost obviously) and first world one. India fits perfectly to this profile and that shows how India draws that much attention.

In addition to that, as it sometimes hard to argue with the numbers according to the study made by Donna Fluss (2005) while the hourly rates vary around $60 in the

---

[10] Saxena, Business Process Outsourcing for Strategic Advantage, 2009, p.4
[11] Oecd, Economic Surveys: India, 2011, p.73
[12] Trent, R. J., & Roberts, L. R. ,*Managing global supply and risk: Best practices, concepts, and strategies*, 2010, p.44

United States it remains at $13 to $18 in India. This big difference in terms of pricing is always due to a huge competitiveness in the country itself. Actually while international firms are looking for expanding their businesses by outsourcing, local companies in India (service providers) are also going through the same situation. As the demand is growing each year in India, service providers are doing their best to stay ahead of the "game". According to Bharat Vagadia (2007), in order to have a viable strategy, domestic outsourcing companies in India are taking into account quality and performance by "specializing their services"[13].

While the others are prey to doubts, the Europeans companies are dancing. Due to this hard competitiveness, they have now an incredible ease of finding their specialized service provider.

3. Ease of finding a service provider

In fact, the tremendous growth of India's IT industry falls in this perspective. According to the Indian economy report [14] the average growth rate of IT industry is "around 36% from 1999-2000 to 2006-2007". This constant growth will enable many European companies to have a wide choice of finding the right service provider for their business. As shown before, the provider is now pushed to specialize his services because of hard competitiveness and make them better and better. This accounts for the fact that India is now considered as a heaven on earth for IT outsourcing. Furthermore, most of these IT outsourcing are conducted in English.

4. Language proficiency

According to the BBC magazine (2016), "the most reliable estimate" is that around 10% of the whole population speaks English which represents approximately 155 million people. For Cyrill Eltschinger (2007) English proficiency "makes the business world go round" [15]. India is now focusing on learning English from a very young age

---

[13] Bharat Vagadia, Outsourcing to India - A Legal Handbook, 2007, p. 16
[14] Vagadia, B. *Outsourcing to India - a legal handbook*, 2007, p. 16
[15] Eltschinger, C., *Source code China: The new global hub of IT outsourcing*, 2007, p. 84

as National University of Education (2012) reports that the number of Indian studying English medium school has increased by 274% from 2003 to 2011.

As shown above, India put all odds on its side to be considered the largest outsourcing provider for IT services. However, the main concern of this study is to understand the factors leading to succeed an IT outsourcing project in India.

Gandhi said (1869-1948), "A nation's culture resides in the hearts and in the soul of its people." In fact, considering working with people from India without taking care of the communication intercultural aspect could stand in the way of European companies' success.

c. Intercultural communication efficiency

This part of the study will be focusing on the importance of intercultural communication in achieving a successful IT outsourcing project in India. This section will be divided into two parts: internal cross-cultural communication within an organization and the external one between the outside world and the service provider. In fact, working within a company without taking into account the internal communication aspect could make companies think that Hell really exists. According to Bernard A. Nijstad (2009) internal communication is "necessary for high team performance"[16].

1. Internal cross-cultural communication

Despite having a high quality staff, the outcome of a project might be disrupted because of a lack of chemistry in the team. Bernard A. Nijstad (2009) made clear the fact that poor internal communication is a barrier and may "undermine cohesion" and due to that team's performance. In order to improve this communication aspect in a cross-cultural context, words play an important role. Indeed, communication is the exchanging of information by speaking, writing or using some other medium (*Oxford Dictionary*) but could also be either verbal or non verbal. According to Randy

---

[16] Nijstad, B. A., *Group performance*, 2009, p.16

Fujishin (2007), "cultures can differ in their communication styles", by the way words are expressing themselves [17].

i. Communication style

Randy Fujishin (2007) considers that communication style is divided into a high context communication and a low context one. A low-context communication is seen as a "message content oriented", taking care more about what was said and where the words are "supremely important". On the contrary, a high-context communication is where "you are expected to understand the implicit rules and unspoken rituals of the culture"[17]. This type of communication might need a better understanding of the culture itself and to read between the lines. According to Sander Schroevers (2013) India has a high context communication style and focus more on the body language than on the words. It shows that if not considering these communication nuances, team will be affected and could in a long-term basis lead to failure within an organization. In reality, from a different culture perspective understanding non-verbal Indian behaviors might be significantly helpful to succeed in working in India. Larry Samovar, Richard Porter and Edwin McDaniel (2014) quote numerous examples of Indian's behaviors; these are few of them:

- Hand holding: While it might be seen by a European culture as a sexual interest Indians consider that more like friendship.
- Yes and no communication: Indian often says yes by shaking their heads sideways, a way that could be considered by a European culture like a no.

Larry Samovar (2014) by its study indicates that this type of behavior are "unconscious" and if not understood could lead to "unsuccessful negotiation, demotivation" and even an "overall climate"[18]. Being from a different culture and working within an Indian organization without taking into consideration these points may result in failing to communicating in an effective way. On the contrary, having a better understanding of these points could make things easier for the employee and

---

[17] Fujishin, R., *Creating effective groups: The art of small group communication*, 2007, p.9
[18] Samovar, L.A., Porter, R. E., & McDaniel, E. R. *Intercultural communication: A reader.* , 2014, p. 174

for his Indian colleagues. As Edward T.Hall (1998) said, "We should never denigrate any other culture but rather help people to understand the relationship between their own culture and the dominant culture".

Consequently, relationship building within an Indian organization is a way to perform internally in a better way. For Richard R. Gesteland and Mary C. Gesteland (2010), India is more relationship focused than deal focused and they point out the fact that Indians are more into building a rapport first before making any deal. So, how important relationship building is for improving your internal cross-cultural communication?

ii. Relationship building

Richard R. Gesteland and Mary C. Gesteland (2010) gave their view on the cultural distance in relationship building between West and India [19]. For them, India stands as an extreme relationship focused culture next to Korea, Japan and China. For this reason, focusing on relationship building while working within an indian company should be seriously taken into account. Randy Fujishin (2007) calls it affection as he considers this relationship at work as a way to better enjoy your experience. In fact, for him building a relationship could be rewarding for the team chemistry but also for the employee himself. Feeling better would make him even more efficient at work. So, having in mind that relationship building in India is important would enhance without any doubts the company's internal communication and accordingly make things easier to optimize a project's outcome.

Similarly, internal communication in a cross-cultural context is equally important to external communication for leading an IT outsourcing business into success. A.C. Krizan (2010) mentions that if a business is likely to succeed, there should be an "effective internal and external communication"[20].

---

[19] Gesteland, R. R., & Gesteland, M. C, *India: Cross-cultural business behavior: For business people, expatriates and scholars*, 2010, p. 32
[20] Krizan, A., Merrier, P., P. Logan, J., & Williams, K. S, *Business Communication*, 2010, p.3

Working in a cross-cultural environment presumes communicating with different cultures. A.C. Krizan (2010) noticed that each organization has its own culture. Hence communicators must overcome these barriers to achieve their business goals [21]. The author gave a simple communication model to illustrate these facts.

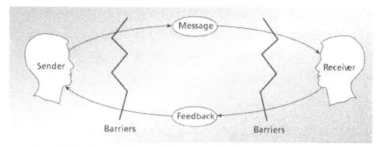

Figure 3.3.2. : Communication model in a cross-cultural context

In this particular case, the communication actors are the outsourcer and the outsourcee. In order to be successful, this communication process needs to overcome these cultural barriers. In addition to that, working in this kind of environment requires from both communication actors' (the outsourcer and the outsourcee) side a kind of warranty in terms of quality and expected results. According to Nannette Rundle CARROLL (2010), not being clear from the beginning of a project could result in poor "organization time, quality results and causes waste of money and harm relationships" [22].

i. Setting-up clear expectations

Before understanding how clear expectations impact a project's outcome, it is important to focus first on what according to studies the major expectations are. This research will be focusing on an IT outsourcing project.

---

[21] Krizan, A., Merrier, P., P. Logan, J., & Williams, K. S, *Business Communication*, 2010, p.9
[22] Carroll, N. R., *The communication problem solver: Simple tools and techniques for busy managers*, 2010, p.23

Stefanie Leimeister (2010) in her investigation noticed that there are four categories of client's expectations [23] in an IT outsourcing context:

- "Business efficiency clients": this type of customers are more focused on achieving "business-related benefits" as they have more concerned about improving their product quality while reducing their costs.
- "Cost-conscious smart shoppers": for these clients reducing costs is their main motive forgetting sometimes to take into fact the possible risk of poor quality.
- "Strategists and innovation seekers": These ones are more into innovation and seek for a high quality team to perform their services.
- "IT excellence": Clients who are seeking for high-skilled people and might have a hard time to find the one by outsourcing.

After having reviewed the major types of client's expectations in the IT outsourcing industry by taking as a support Stefanie Leimeister's (2010) investigation, let's take a look on how important great expectations might affect an IT outsourcing project end result.

In fact, "expectations are understood as the anticipated or estimated behavior and precede the perceived outcome or performance of a relationship" (Churchill/Surprenant 1982). Stefanie Leimeister (2010) considers that before starting contracting out to an outsourcing company, the need to make sure that all the requirements, contract clauses, team management are agreed by both parties is greater than ever to succeed. She actually sees this point as a "theoretical pillar" of IT outsourcing success.

This kind of actions has also to be performed throughout the project by giving feedbacks as much as possible. A.C. Krizan (2010) considers that giving a constructive

---

[23] Leimeister, S., *IT outsourcing governance: Client types and their management strategies.* . 2010, p.156

feedback on a relevant concern at a time might affect the desired result [24]. He points out the fact that many contractors while communicating are giving vague feedbacks and by that are not helping communication to work out efficiently. Of course it is import to manage client's expectations before and during the project's progress, but making sure that this relationship lasts as long as possible is the key for a long term working relation.

ii. Client relationship building

"No company can succeed without customers. If you don't have customers you don't have a business. "(Don Peppers and Martha Rogers, 2010). Ensuring a good relationship building with your clients is a major factor to keep your customers and then make your business work in a long-term basis. Don Peppers and Martha Rogers (2010) consider that building this relationship helps companies to "keep, get and grow customers"[25]. By growing a customer, he will in a natural way bring additional work; ensure word-of-mouth benefits and then keep saving more operational costs. By keeping them, he will "retain profitable customer longer" and "eliminate" the unprofitable ones. The authors consider that a customer is not profitable when the management time is far too important in comparison with the project's size[25].

However, sometimes the relationship between contractors is not well balanced according to Charles M. Vance and Yongsun Paik (2006). For them, in a more multicultural environment there is always one dominating the other. This kind of companies' relationship is subject to conflicts and could break at any time. Many aspects are due to this issue but are not in the scope of this research.

As shown in previous chapters, IT outsourcing industry in India is really competitive and in order to survive, companies have to find other ways than reducing their cost and their quality service. According to Martha Rogers (2010), companies use

---

[24] Krizan, A., Merrier, P., P. Logan, J., & Williams, K. S, *Business Communication*, 2010, p.376

[25] Peppers, D., & Rogers, *Managing customer relationships: A strategic framework*, 2010, chapter 1: Evolution of relationships with customers

information to gain a competitive advantage among all the other service providers. By information she meant a CRM (customer relationship management) system in order to get closer to their customer and ensure a smooth transition.

Giving a definition of CRM (Customer relationship management) might be as hard as defining what IT is in a sentence. Its definition might be easier if applied in a particular context. Hedman and Kalling (2002) gave a clearer definition of this concept as a tool for IT-based marketing that helps companies manage their relationships. Implementing a CRM, in an IT based context, is a good way to keep track of all the information and ensure in case of staff addition or even enterprise downsizing a smooth transition. Annekie Brink and Adele Berndt (2009) pointed out the fact that in a multicultural environment, transition has to be "treated" like a project and CRM helps that if implementing it. However, according to a survey made by Mairaj Salim and Sanman Jain N (n.d), only 19% of Indian organizations (including IT outsourcing companies) use a complete CRM system but expected to grow since 2006 at an annual rate of 40%. Indian companies started to understand that having this CRM is nowadays mandatory to manage customers as effective as possible. In fact, M. Woog (2009) considers a CRM as a "competitive advantage" to better understand the customer's needs, where change within an organization is nowadays a "central element"[26]. Since the world is in constant change, some things might be subject to evolve and knowledge is one of these.

d. Technology knowledge

This chapter will be focusing on how important technology knowledge is to succeed in a fast-moving IT outsourcing world. This section aims at understanding how knowledge has to be integrated to ensure a long-term viable strategy.

---

[26] Woog, M., *Change Management according to a CRM implementation*, 2009, p.1

Defining what knowledge is would take ages, as "knowledge of what is does not open the door directly to what should be"(Einstein Albert, 1939). Even if India has one of the largest talent communities worldwide[27], this talent has to be used the right way.

1. Adaptable IT staff

To stay ahead of the game, IT outsourcing companies need a qualified adaptable staff. According to Randy E Cadieux (2014), employees have to be able to "adapt to change environment"[28]. This adaptation could lead the employee to have a different position within the company. In an IT outsourcing context, having to understand or learn a new technology might be considered as one of these changes according to the same author. It requires from the team's side a "power" as they are getting now out of their comfort zone. Doing something that they were not used to do will benefit to the outsourcing organization itself and to the outsourcer. According to Albert Plugge's (2012) study in an IT outsourcing company in India, doing only tasks without thinking out of the box might not be the best solution for company's future [29]. This IT outsourcing company has a slogan, which is "from running client's business to changing client's business". For the same author, in a long-term basis there is a need to find people with a capability to propose solutions and not only doing what they used to do. Referring to the same company and in order to achieve this goal, they introduced a program that they called "Employee first". In this program, they create facilities to enhance innovation and make their employees feel better, almost like home. By taking care of this aspect, they will put more effort in the balance and consequently improve the company's competitiveness by giving ideas and solutions. The author pointed out that employees are the company's main assets, and finding "thinkers" or making them is the best strategy to differentiate themselves from the market. For Hans-Werner Franz, Josef Hochgerner and Jürgen Howaldt (2012) added

---

[27] Saxena, K. B., & Bharadwaj, S. S., *Business process outsourcing: For strategic advantage*, 2007, p.4
[28] Cadieux, R. E. (2014). *Team leadership in high-hazard environments: Performance, safety and risk management strategies for operational teams*, 2014, p.180
[29] Robert-Ribes, J., *Connecting forward: Advanced networking for executives changing jobs, company, industry or country*, 2012, p.4

value should not be technology centered but has to take into consideration social innovations. By this latter they meant improving "quality of life" and employees' daily activities.

However, even if innovation is a great added value in an IT outsourcing company, employees must go hand in hand with the times as new technologies are born nowadays. As a result, developers must be able to adapt quickly to new languages while having a strong basis of the previous ones [30].

2. Knowledge sharing

In fact, for this reason John Child and Martin Ihrig (2013) consider that knowledge needs to be transmitted in a regular basis. In reality, this knowledge sharing can be either internally (within the company) or externally (between both contractors) [31]. These two if combined, according to Lee (2001) is one of "major predictor of outsourcing success. He emphasizes the fact that both sides could learn by working together to improve their management processes in particular. However, the main challenge for outsourcing company is continuity. For Vivek Sharma (2012) this continuity is related to creating a strategic partnership. According to his study, western companies "are increasingly looking for Indian IT outsourcing companies as strategic partners".

e. Creating a strategic partnership

In the last chapter of this theoretical study, there will be a focus on the fact that creating a strategic partnership in the IT outsourcing world is significantly important for a long-term continuity. According to Vivek Sharma (2009), Indian and European companies are able to cross their knowledge by forming a partnership and by that improve themselves. However for Gordon B. Baty, Michael Blake (1990), a strategic partnership could work only if both parties share the same vision. They give

---

[30] Morley, D., & Parker, C. S. , *Understanding computers: Today and tomorrow: Comprehensive.* 2012, p.419
[31] Chu, S., Ritter, W., & Al-Hawamdeh, S. *Managing knowledge for global and collaborative innovations*, 2010, p.43

a practical example as they compare it to marriage. For them "as in a marriage there are a lot more ways for things to go wrong than for things to go right".

From the very beginning of an IT outsourcing project, it is vital to seek the same goals. Matthew T. Hora (2011) points out the fact that the main attribute for a successful partnership is the alignment of both parties' objectives.

1. Goals aligned

On the section related to "Setting-up clear expectations", the research made by Stefanie Leimeister (2010) shows that there were different types of clients in term of expectations. Some were seeking for a high quality staff meanwhile some others were just looking for the cheapest service provider. Consequently, before creating any partnership it is important to know whether or not the outsourcee is able to respond to the customer's needs.

2. Commitment

According to Matthew T. Hora (2010), it is mandatory not to give false promises. For him, many IT outsourcing companies are committing to projects that they are not even able to perform. This is for him due to the fact that IT outsourcing companies are more looking for securing a long-term continuity but in fact this relation is counterproductive and could be conflicting. For Matthew T. Hora (2010) it is what "erodes the trust". For him, trust plays a central role in partnerships.

3. Trust

When there is not trust, there is no partnership. For Matthew T. Hora and Susan Bolyard Millar (2010), "trust is developed incrementally and over time". By this fact, it is not possible to create a trust at the very first stage of a project but after many successful months or even years of work. For these authors, trust is an accumulation of commitments and goals' alignments over a certain amount of time. In the IT outsourcing context, trust might be one of the most difficult thing to gain from outsourcers. As European companies have an ease to find potential outsourcing service providers, this could at any time and for any reason break contracting with them.

In this chapter, we answered the major factors that lead an IT outsourcing project to succeed raised by researches. The factors discussed during this chapter are:

- Intercultural communication: In this section, we explained how important internal and external communication in a multicultural environment impacts a project's outcome in an IT outsourcing company.
- Knowledge integration: This section gives an overview of how to integrate knowledge in order to perform better within a company and with the outside world.
- Creating partnerships is also a key for a successful IT outsourcing project in case of alignment of goals, commitment and trust between both sides (the outsourcer and the outsourcee)

However from the theoretical side, the difference between theory and practice is small but in practice it is very large. Consequently, my thesis will compare the theoretical base to my related experience in an IT outsourcing company in India.

IV. Result and analysis

a. Introduction

This part of the study will be supported by my 6 months' IT outsourcing experience in India. By the permission of the CEO, the company's name will be disclosed. As a reminder, Helios Solutions is an IT outsourcing company founded in 1999 that has a particularity comparing to the other service providers: it works exclusively for the European market.

In this chapter, I will make a comparison between the IT outsourcing experience I have lived through and the theoretical framework. For that reason, I will go over four main points:

- The intercultural internal communication
- The external communication in a cross-cultural context
- Technology knowledge adaptation
- Creating a strategic partnership

By gathering this data, I will make an analysis to find out the points that need to be optimized at Helios Solutions in a future basis. The part of this study is linked to my experience and cannot under any circumstances be considered as an absolute truth.

b. Facing the internal communication challenge

During this experience, there were 6 project managers coming from Germany, France, The Netherlands and Norway. They all had to work in a different environment and accordingly they needed to get out of their comfort zone. Actually, working in a cross-cultural environment requires most of the times an aptitude to change and to adapt to a different mindset and organization structure.

For an intern who did not really have any relevant experience in the past, having to manage different projects with a high responsibility constitutes an important challenge. In this part, I will be particularly focusing on the internal communication challenge that I experienced within Helios Solutions.

- English proficiency at Helios Solutions

The first thing I wanted to highlight is English proficiency. According to the theoretical background, many researches have shown that India's second language is English, a language spoken by almost 10% of the population. However, there were not any relevant studies that gather information related to the English level within Indian companies. Consequently, I will give firstly my personal impression and then support it by the interview I had with the company's project manager.

English in India is sometimes hard to be understood because of its strong accent. I did not really escape from the rule at the very beginning of my experience as I had a hard time understanding what developers wanted to say.

These are from my experience the points that sometimes made the communication within the company difficult.

- o Indians not only speak fast but also involve their accent, which makes usually more difficult to understand and to be understood
- o "W" letter does not sound like a W in Indian mouths but more like a V.
- o Swallowing words

These are some examples I still have in mind and that really draw my attention. However, understanding a new accent requires time. After 3 weeks, I was able to understand and got used to this new accent. Even though, there were still miscommunication problems that occurred but this time not from my side. There were two types of English miscommunication that I mainly faced:

- o Poor English skills: This time even after getting used to this new accent, it was almost impossible to understand some developers. They were trying their best to express themselves and to explain a particular situation, but they have a limited English proficiency for that. This sometimes led to a great waste of time for communication to take place. For this purpose, I needed to ask an Indian colleague to ensure that everything was understood perfectly. In some cases, the developers did not go straight to the point because of the same reasons mentioned above. And this explains the lack of motivation to carry on the communication process. To better understand this point, I will give a concrete example. We had to create a website for one French client and it needed from the developer's side to code one section. The problem was that if the client started updating his website all the changes made by the developer will be gone. For this reason and because I was not informed, we wasted too much time and this had an impact on the project's progress. As a result, we were not able to deliver it on time. These small miscommunication problems have a big influence on the project's outcome.
- o "Yes" and "No" dilemma: Even when some developers did not understand a point, they used to say that they do. From my side, thinking that everything was understood led sometimes to bad surprises. For instance, I made one task

document and went through all the requirements with one developer. It seemed that everything was in order but because of a lack of communication, some points were not fully understood. Some tasks needed to be done again and led to slow down the project's progress.

To support the result of this case study, I had an interview with Helios Solutions' websites project manager Akash Soni regarding the level of English used by his team and how it had an impact on their performance. I chose Akash Soni as he is the one who keeps in touch with most of the developers on a regular basis and has this position for more than 9 years.

He considers that around 15 out of 101 developers are speaking English fluently and by this fact has never reported any problems from their side. The rest of them have a basic level of English but are able to understand the requirements. However, few of them had a hard time speaking with international project managers because of their lack of experience. Akash Soni by his experience thinks that this problem will be resolved with time and developers with a bad level will improve year in and year out. He points out that among the developers with an intermediate level of English, 90% were not able to speak a word two years back. So for him, his English team's level is improving and has absolutely nothing to envy to company's competitors.

From his point of view, the most important thing in a project's process is to understand clients' requirements. The only person in charge of this task at the very beginning of a project is the international project manager. He has to gather information from clients and pass them to developers. The diagram below illustrates these processes.

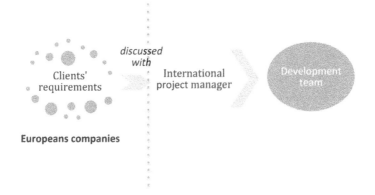

Figure 4.2: Communication process model of Helios Solutions

According to Akash Soni, the discussion between the client and the international project manager, if not performed well, could lead to big misunderstanding. He stated that during his 9 years as a project manager at Helios Solutions, this issue happened quite often. For him, English is important to bridge the communication gap between European companies and Helios Solutions but is not the main factor behind the success of an IT outsourcing project.

However, he pointed out that to face this kind of issue, the only thing to do is to get involved in the clients' discussion processes. This solution would resolve the problem, as he would make sure from the clients' side that all the requirements are understood.

As far as I am concerned, this solution might not be the best for Helios Solutions, as it will not be performed in a long-term basis. Project managers like Akash Soni are really busy with other projects and are not ready to be involved in all the discussions processes.

This interview emphasizes the fact that English is important for communicating throughout the project's progress but a perfect understanding is needed at its very first stage. If the requirements are not clearly understood from the international project manager's side, this could lead to misunderstandings and impact considerably the project's outcome.

However, even if the requirements are perfectly understood, there are still some intercultural communication aspects that need to be seriously taken into consideration. From my experience, at the beginning I was struggling to understand some Indian behaviors. One of these is their communication style.

- Communication style and relationship building

The theoretical framework has shown that the communication style is related to culture. According to the same source, India has a high context communication style, as the people are more using their body to interact. In fact, non-verbal communication is more predominant than the verbal one.

After few days working in India, the first thing that I noticed is the way people were interacting with each other. I actually discovered it when I had a face to face with the CEO for the first time. In fact, this day was my first day at Helios Solutions and I was asking him some questions related to this new experience in India. He was always answering by shaking his head sideways, meaning the opposite. While Western people consider it as a "no", it does mean "yes" for Indians. From this point in time, I knew that I had to face something completely new.

When I had to communicate for the first time with developers, something drew particularly my attention. They were really shy and reserved, almost intimidated when I had a first talk with them. The communication did not really seem natural and I felt that I was a burden to them. For this reason, I had to find a way to break this barrier in order to make the communication work more natural. You are certainly asking yourself how this impacts a project's progress and I will provide the answer to this question.

Without taking into considering the human aspect in an internal organization, no communication will occur. Nothing can be performed without any communication. I was in a hot country but the atmosphere was really cold. In reality, to overcome these barriers, you have to create a relationship with your workers. This relationship building might be from my experience the only way to have the best working atmosphere. Developers in a natural way will make things easier for you and will not be scared to tell you if something goes wrong.

As an example, I was working with one developer and right at the beginning of the project, it was really hard to communicate with him. It was actually not due to language issues but more to the bad atmosphere. After weeks, I tried to make things easier for both of us by communicating with him after official work. This kind of behavior created a sort of relationship and made afterwards the communication easier.

If I have learned anything about communication in this cross-cultural context in my six months internship, it is that relationship building is the central point. From my experience, I noticed that creating trust and then making communication easier is related to building a personal relationship. Obviously not with all your team workers, but a good communication come with trust, credibility and reliability.

To support my experience, a developer accepted to answer my questions. Due to confidentiality issues, his/her name will not be disclosed. For easiness of the reader, this person will be called X.

X has been working at Helios Solutions for more than five years and worked with more than fifteen international project managers. The following part is a summary related to our talk.

Right before working with any international project manager, X is always observing the behavior of his co-worker. He considers that his behavior will affect the way he will be interacting with him in the future. X does not view that like preconceived ideas but from his experience noticed that some internationals looked down on him. For his point of view, they underestimate the fact that they are from a different culture and that theirs is of greater value. So because of that, he would not make any effort to build a positive atmosphere. The illustration below explains this phenomenon.

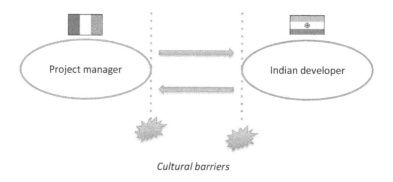

Cultural barriers

Figure 4.2: Communication barriers in a cross-cultural environment

In reality, from both sides there are perceived ideas that impact the internal communication efficiency. Most of the time, this common phenomenon creates miscommunication cultural barriers.

For this reason, X considers that building relationship is a way of breaking up these barriers. However, according to him the internal communication process could also be efficient if the relation is completely professional. For him, building a relationship improves the communication process, which optimizes the project's outcome but is not in any case mandatory for succeeding an IT outsourcing project.

In conclusion, according to my point of view and to the interview I have had with X, it is obvious that understanding and accepting someone's culture is important. Someone willing to work in a multicultural environment needs obviously to adapt himself to different situations. In addition, seen the theoretical studies and my own experience, relationship building is a central point for an IT outsourcing project to be successful but X disagrees with this point. He considers that this factor is only optimizing the project's end result and has not to be considered as a major point, in any case.

To counter these issues at Helios Solutions, there should be an informative training for new international project managers to understand these cultural nuances. As it is from both sides, developers have to understand that western countries have also a different communication style and mindset. Understanding both communication styles would certainly avoid this issue.

Having studied the internal communication issue faced at Helios Solutions, the next part will be mainly focused on the importance of external communication in an IT outsourcing project.

c. Importance of external communication

From my own experience, having an efficient external communication is a key for a successful project. A project always starts by setting up clear expectations to the client. Indeed, the customer has to be sure that his project is under the outsourcee's scope of work and that all the terms of the contract has been agreed on. This very first stage of the project has to be taken seriously into consideration to avoid any conflict throughout the project's progress. However, due to cultural differences many contradictory things may happen. When I had a meeting with developers, we were mainly talking about the feasibility of a project before starting doing it. The problem was that they used to say in a first place that the project is doable and few days after having settled an oral agreement with the client, they changed their mind. This kind of behavior is related to the "yes" and "no" dilemma that was mentioned previously. The issue is that behaving this way leads to lose trust in outsourcing in this company. In addition, this attitude is unprofessional and most of the time pushes the outsourcer to stop dealing with Helios Solutions.

During this experience, I had to manage twelve projects (not at the same time obviously) with different clients' expectations, which will be shown in the chart below:

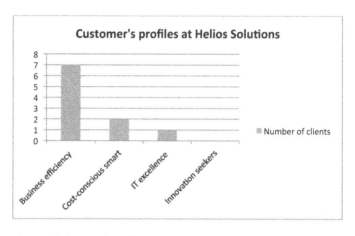

Figure 4.3: Customer's profiles at Helios Solutions

- Seven "business efficiency" clients: This constitutes the main part of Helios Solutions' clients as they look for the best value for money.

- Two "Cost-conscious smart shoppers": They were looking for the cheapest and were trying to bargain for getting some discounts. One of these two clients was used to work with Helios Solutions for more than four years and chose to outsource in Pakistan for lower prices.

- One "IT excellence" client: I had to manage a project with one client who was looking for perfection. He was looking for a pixel perfect website and seeking for a high quality product.

A client's profile is related to his expectations. From my experience, working with an "IT excellence" client was not possible. He had really high expectations and it was hard to respond to his needs. For this reason, the collaboration ended after only two months. The fact that he was not really kind did not really help and made the atmosphere of work difficult.

34

As far as I am concerned, "IT excellence" clients are not in Helios Solutions' scope. I think that this type of clients have also to understand that having a perfect result with lower prices might not be feasible by outsourcing. By giving this example, it shows that even by having a perfect understanding of all the requirements, and by making sure that the internal communication is done well, the expected outcome is quite often opposite to reality. For this reason, this is mandatory to classify clients according to their requirements in order to make sure that a project is feasible.

As a contribution to my practical research, Ashish Sharma business developer at Helios Solutions accepted to give his thoughts on the importance of external communication within an organization. His answers were related to his experience at Helios Solutions.

For him, external communication is important as it involves existing, potential and former clients. For him, they all have a role to optimize the external communication efficiency.

- A former client is someone who you used to work with but for some reasons stop working with you. This type of clients is the most important because they help you to progress in a future basis thanks to their feedbacks. They actually point out some points that went wrong in order not to do them again.
- You need to keep the existing client as they are the ones who are running the company
- Find a way to attract new potential clients.

According to Ashish Sharma, external communication is the major point to succeed in outsourcing. The companies you are working with are judging you by your ability to perform a good external communication. They do not see what happens within your company. Even if things are not working well internally, the image Helios Solutions is reflecting towards its clients is important.

We had a talk about the importance of setting up clear expectations at the very beginning of the project. From his point of view, these expectations have to be reviewed not only at the beginning but also throughout the project's progress. The diagram above illustrates his thoughts.

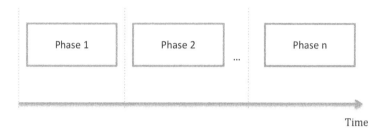

Figure 4.3: Expectations throughout project phases

Before starting a project, a client comes with all his requirements and the development team assesses its feasibility. This first feasibility assessment has a great importance as it includes all the clients' needs. By this feasibility analysis, we know whether or not we are able to deliver this kind of project. However, most of the time a client comes up with new ideas and accordingly new things to implement. These new requirements have also to be evaluated by the technical team after every change requests. So, by the support of Ashish Sharma, setting-up expectations has to be done not only at the very first stage of a project but also during its realization.

In reality, failing at providing clients clear expectations can seriously impact your relationship with them. We all know that without customers, there is no business. So, taking care of your existing clients and building a good relationship is vital for a long-term work. According to what I experienced at Helios Solutions, keeping clients for a long-term basis was quite hard and it was mainly due to the fact that there was a change of international project managers every six months. I think that for this reason there is a need to ensure a smooth transition.

Helios Solutions have an added value compared to their competitors. Clients can interact with project managers in their native tongue and it facilitates the communication process. This way of transacting creates trust in the clients and as a consequence it makes them work more efficiently. However, when the client is used to work with an international project manager and this latter has to leave after six months, it is obvious that it impacts considerably the project's end result. I actually lived through the same situation, as the previous project manager entrusted me with many initiated projects. I had a hard time managing and understanding projects that had already started. In fact, if the transition is not made smoothly, that could have a big influence on the project's outcome. From my own experience, this transition has to be done in a better way to avoid these issues.

According to Ashish Sharma, creating a CRM system is a solution to face this issue and ensure a smooth transition. The problem was that the CRM system used at Helios Solutions was really old-fashioned and bugging all the time. Besides, this system was not providing all the information needed in order to have an overview of the projects' progress.

After our discussion Ashish Sharma considered this point and asked for updating this system. The solution given might be implemented at Helios Solutions in a future basis to ensure a better understanding of on-going projects for new project managers. The new project manager by gathering all this information will be in a better position to manage efficiently his clients' projects. Moreover, the client will not feel that any transition has been made and thus the project would be carried on naturally. Moreover, another solution that has also to be taken into account is to involve the new international project manager into the conversation processes before he starts working within the company. Right after he got hired for the position, he needs to know the number of projects he will be managing and get all the documents needed to understand each of them. By using this technique, the new international project manager will have time to digest all this new information. I actually faced this issue when I first started working at Helios Solutions. Even if the former project manager gave me a good training and an overview of all the project's progress, it was still hard to process all the data. I needed more than two weeks to know perfectly what all the projects were about. This time could be optimized by using these techniques and ensure a perfect transition.

Not only that, a client to feel more comfortable needs to be informed in a regular basis of the project's progress. Indeed, as the client is outsourcing in India, he cannot take a trip down there to see how things are going on. It is mandatory to keep client in touch of everything that has been implemented within the company to create trust and make him feel that there is no distance between him and the outsourcing company.

At Helios Solutions, every project is divided into phases and at the end of each of them there is a release. I used to share a document with my clients to inform them in a regular basis about the project's advancement. Even if the work is done perfectly and the client is not informed by the task being performed, he would not feel confident in outsourcing in this company. Reporting a state of a project is for all these reasons, mandatory and if not done can lead to misunderstandings (due to a lack of communication) as some parts could be misunderstood at the project's very first stage or even throughout the project's progress.

In addition, time is a constraint for most outsourcers. For this reason, releasing a project on time is mandatory for a project's success, to say the least. At almost every meeting I attended, the point that has been discussed the most is when the project will be delivered. Not meeting this requirement could lead to break the collaboration even if the work and the communication throughout the project has been done perfectly.

For Ashish Sharma, in this competitive world, the success rate of an IT outsourcing project is below forty percent that's why efforts have to be joined to maintain existing clients. To be on the safe side, you need to ensure that nothing has to be left to chance.

For this reason, we will focus on another main aspect of making an IT outsourcing project successful: Technology knowledge.

d. Technology knowledge

From my point of view, it is imperative to master a technology or a language in IT programming. However, this knowledge has to be used accurately to ensure a long-term viability of a company.

Helios Solutions has a large team of developers working in many technologies. For this reason, I will take as an example the number of developers working with a CMS. As a reminder, a CMS is a content management system that is used to create websites. Some CMS are more difficult than others and this is related to their functionalities. I will not go into details, as it is not the scope of my thesis. The chart below shows the number of developers for each CMS technology.

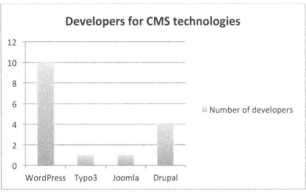

Figure 4.4 : Developers according to their CMS technology

According to the chart, we can see that the WordPress developers are the most outstanding in comparison to the other types of CMS technologies' developers. It represents 62,5% of the whole process of the CMS technologies at Helios Solutions.

Something that drew my attention while working at Helios Solutions is that the number of WordPress developers is greater compared to the requirements of the market. Indeed, the WordPress business is decreasing through time and this is due to the fact that creating a WordPress website does no longer require a substantial know-how but it can be conducted by a common person, not necessarily having high qualifications in this technology. From what I have lived through, I noticed that out of ten developers, many did not fulfill the eight effective required working hours. Consequently, a lot of precious time is wasted and could be positively optimized for better work productivity. That's why we need a coherent collaborative teamwork.

From my own experience, there were four Drupal developers working full time. This number was not enough, as we needed one additional resource developer in this company. Therefore, this latter opted for hiring an experienced Drupal developer to achieve the working tasks waiting ahead. I think this procedure was not efficient in the sense that the company was mainly thinking about the ultimate result instead of having a long-term vision. As a matter of fact, the ten WordPress developers did not work eight effective hours per day, which was a waste of time and could have been used more rationally in other CMS technologies. All this wasted time might have being beneficial for Drupal team and would have avoided financial loss to the company.

To remedy this situation, I recommend that in the future companies like Helios Solutions think ahead of time and should have a long-term vision in the IT resource management industry. For this reason, they should use their existing staff to fulfill the working tasks instead of hiring experienced employees for a particular technology. As an example, getting experienced in Drupal for a WordPress developer requires time but in the long run we need to predict the future and compensate the lack of employees in Drupal development by Helios Solutions' own resources.

To highlight the idea above, let me give a concrete example, which will be shown, in the illustration below. The numbers being used might be subject to change.

Real time ratio for WordPress and Drupal

Ratio (effective time/daily
contractual working time)

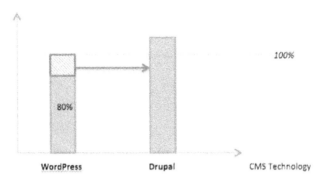

Figure 4.4: Real time ratio for WordPress and Drupal

As we can see in the chart above, the ratio (effective time divided by the daily contractual working time of eight hours) equals to 80% for WordPress technology. It means that in average 20% of each developer is wasting this time by not working. In the other side, the ratio for Drupal is more than 100% and the 20% of WordPress ratio could compensate this lack.

Assuming that 20% of the time being used by the WordPress developers is wasted ineffectively, two developers out of ten do not carry out their task, taking into consideration that eight of the developers work full time (which means having a ratio of 1 or more than 1).

As a suggestion, two of the ten developers should delegate some of their tasks to the WordPress team to fill in relatively the missing eight daily-required working hours. By doing this, they would compensate the loss time and collaborate with the Drupal team. Therefore, their respective developers would gain experience by being assisted by Drupal developers. This is what we call knowledge sharing, which actually should be used in a more collaborative and efficient way.

From my point of view, a better knowledge of the market needs helps us anticipate and have a clear vision on how to use efficiently our resources. Therefore, time is used in an optimal way and tasks are shared accordingly between all IT developers.

Among all the people that I have to deal with and that I actually interviewed, Akash Soni seemed to me the best representation of this topic for my research paper. Akash Soni used to be a software developer before he became a project manager at Helios Solutions. That is the reason why I chose him as he has a complete knowledge of the mechanism of internal team development.

For him, the developers are the biggest assets in a company and making sure that they are qualified is a major point for performing high quality products. According to him, every developer has to master one particular technology in order to deliver the best work. He did actually consider that a developer has to be specialized in only one CMS technology field but did not really think about the future. If one day, a CMS like WordPress is no longer used, what are they supposed to do? Akash Soni said that to counter that, these latters would get trained for another technology. The problem is that waiting till a technology is no longer needed by clients would cause a big waste of time for the company and "time is money".

During his nine years as a project manager, Akash Soni had some projects' requests of technologies that are not developed by Helios Solutions. To face this issue and to respond to the customers' needs, Helios Solutions outsources this work to an external party in case the outsourcer is a big client that will provide him in a future basis additional work. They are investing even with a really small margin (hourly rate margin) in order to get new clients. This way of doing things is risky but can also lead Helios Solutions to attract more customers. It can seem strange for everyone but outsourcing companies in India are also outsourcing their services in order to grow.

After that, we had a talk about the fact that some technologies are in a decline. For him, it is business developers' and marketing team's work to bring projects and it is really rare that a web technology disappears. In the case WordPress is no longer requested, he suggested that the development team in charge of this technology would be needed any longer. Helios Solutions would eventually, if need be, hire someone specialized in this "new" technology to respond to the market needs.

He did not mention the fact whether the existing team is liable and able to do the job properly. We cannot fire people with high skills just because they are not experienced in a particular technology. The thing to do is to use your own resource and not look for an external developer to fill the gap.

In this chapter, thanks to Akash Soni's input and to my six-month experience in an IT outsourcing company, I emphasize the fact that an adaptable team is a key to perform a long-term viability within an organization. In addition, I point out the importance of knowledge sharing to ensure a smooth transition in terms of technology use.

The next and last chapter will be focusing on the importance of creating a strategic partnership and will be supported by the interview I had with Helios Solutions' CEO Jigar Shah.

e. Creating a strategic partnership

Jigar Shah founded Helios Solutions in 1999 and knows the company better than anyone else. For this reason, he would give his thoughts on the importance of creating a strategic partnership for a successful IT outsourcing company. This part of the study will only be backed up by the information I gathered from the CEO and compared to the theoretical base.

He knew that creating an outsourcing company is not an easy thing in such a competitive world. He actually started in 1999 to outsource to some local clients and also to some customers from USA. He noticed that it was hard to keep his existing clients in a long-term basis in the sense that all his competitors were actually doing the same. To remedy this situation, you need also to be creative and find out things that others do not do. This is actually very hard to achieve but Jigar Shah did. He started working in 2006 exclusively for European clients and in addition to that he hired inters from this continent. He started with the Dutch market to extend his business afterwards to the German, French and Norwegian ones. Jigar Shah hired

European interns in order to bridge the cultural and communication gap that Indians might not be capable of.

By all the things he went through as an entrepreneur, Jigar Shah gave me the motives that are for him, the most important for making an IT outsourcing business successful. These are his three key factors for being efficient in the IT outsourcing industry:

- Skilled development team referring to the outsourcing business. Without them nothing could be performed.
- Efficient internal communication
- Very good business relationship with outsourcers

They are equally important and lacking one of these three factors could considerably impact a project's end result. According to the scope of my thesis, we will be mainly focusing on the third key factor Jigar Shah mentioned: maintaining a good relationship with your outsourcers.

For Helios Solutions' CEO, creating a strategic partnership does not require to get any official contract signed between both parties. This has to be more a moral relationship agreement and will for this reason ensure long-term collaboration continuity. This relationship has to be based on respect, commitment and regular assessment:

- Respect: It can seem obvious but for Jigar Shah many companies were outsourcing to Helios Solutions and more considering it like a "sweat shop". This without any doubt affects the team's performance as speaking with someone who lack respect creates a bad atmosphere and for this reason poor working conditions.
- Commitment: Before starting contracting with any companies, you need to make sure that you are able to respond to their needs. These latters can be related to an oral commitment or a contract agreement.
- Regular assessment: After each project's phase or at the end of each project, you need to make sure that the client provides you with a feedback. By this

feedback, you will be able to know the points that went wrong in order to fix them in the future.

The future is actually a matter for all the IT outsourcing companies in India according to Jigar Shah. Succeeding in outsourcing is not an easy thing to do but being able to anticipate the future might help you not to fail afterwards. The labor cost in India in the IT industry is increasing and consequently clients are tempted to outsource elsewhere. For all these reasons mentioned, Helios Solutions has to find a way to stay ahead of this "game" where only the strongest survive.

V.   Conclusion

a.   General overview

All in all, the IT outsourcing business is a complex study field, which requires a lot of parameters and skills in order to be successful and beneficial. That's why my thesis tried to highlight the factors that make of an IT outsourcing enterprise a successful one. But this is sometimes faced with many shortcomings and limitations.

The key factors that are behind a successful IT outsourcing project according to my research scope are:

- An effective internal cross-cultural communication
- A rational external communication
- An adaptable strategy for technology knowledge
- Creating a strategic partnership

Having dealt with all the issues mentioned above, I came to the conclusion that many things are subject to change in Helios Solutions. Therefore, I would like to put forward some recommendations for future use to make the IT outsourcing more successful and efficient.

b.   Recommendations for Helios Solutions

Here are briefly some recommendations relevant to the IT outsourcing in Helios Solutions:

- Continuous assessment for Helios Solutions' IT outsourcing developers in terms of language proficiency and communicative strategy
- International project manager profile: specific training to scope with technical challenges and suggest solutions to overcome unexpected shortcomings and limitations

- Cross-cultural awareness is vital. International project manager should be sensitized as how to deal with cultural differences so as to optimize the internal communication within Helios Solutions
- Reliability of decision making as far as the IT developers and Indian project managers are concerned
- Improving the existing CRM system
- Ensure good and smoother transition between the existing and forthcoming international project manager
- Adapting existing resources to the required technologies and avoiding hiring extra human resources (WP and Drupal case related earlier)
- Sensitizing IT resource developers to the limitations of outsourcing and thinking ahead into the future to find alternatives in order to fight competitiveness: the CEO should find or bring innovation people in who are able to "think out of the box".

c. Propositions for future research

Throughout this entire thesis, I have reflected on many questions that could enhance scientific research in the field of IT outsourcing, which are the following:

- How could we possible overcome cross-cultural differences in the IT outsourcing context?
- What is the future of outsourcing in India?
- Is India able to be a thinking outsourcing country?

Bibliography

Articles and books references

Barrar, P., & Gervais, R. (2006). *Global outsourcing strategies: An international reference on effective outsourcing relationships.* Aldershot, England: Gower.

Baty, G. B., & Blake, M. (2003). *Entrepreneurship: Back to basics.* Washington, D.C.: Beard Books.

Cadieux, R. E. (2014). *Team leadership in high-hazard environments: Performance, safety and risk management strategies for operational teams.* Gower Publishing.

Carroll, N. R. (2010). *The communication problem solver: Simple tools and techniques for busy managers.* New York, NY: American Management Association.

Child, J., & Ihrig, M. (n.d.). *Knowledge, organization, and management: Building on the work of Max Boisot.*

Chu, S., Ritter, W., & Al-Hawamdeh, S. (2010). *Managing knowledge for global and collaborative innovations.* Singapore: World Scientific.

Eltschinger, C. (2007). *Source code China: The new global hub of IT outsourcing.* Hoboken, NJ: John Wiley & Sons.

Franz, H., Hochgerner, J., & Howaldt, J. (2012). *Challenge social innovation: Potentials for business, social entrepreneurship, welfare and civil society.* Heidelberg: Springer.

Fujishin, R. (2007). *Creating effective groups: The art of small group communication.* Lanham: Rowman & Littlefield.

Gesteland, R. R., & Gesteland, M. C. (2010). *India: Cross-cultural business behavior: For business people, expatriates and scholars.* Frederiksberg: Copenhagen Business School Press.

Hall, E. T. (1959). *The silent language.* Garden City, NY: Doubleday.

Halvey, J. K., & Melby, B. M. (1996). *Information technology outsourcing transactions: Process, strategies, and contracts.* New York: Wiley.

Information economy report 2007-2008: Science an technology for development: The new paradigm of ICT. (2007). New York: United Nations.

Jacques, V. (2006). *International outsourcing strategy and competitiveness: Study on current outsourcing trends, IT, business processes, contact centers.* Paris: Publibook.

Krizan, A., Merrier, P., P. Logan, J., & Williams, K. S. (2010). *Business Communication.* Cengage Learning.

Leimeister, S. (2010). *IT outsourcing governance: Client types and their management strategies.* Wiesbaden: Gabler.

Mahnke, V., Overby, M. L., & Vang, J. (2003). *Strategic IT-outsourcing: What do we know and need to know?* Kbh.: Handelshøjskolen i København, Institut for Informatik.

McDonald, K. T. (2010). *Above the clouds: Managing risk in the world of cloud computing.* Ely: IT Governance Publishing.

Morley, D., & Parker, C. S. (2012). *Understanding computers: Today and tomorrow: Comprehensive.* Boston, MA: Course Technology Cengage Learning.

Nijstad, B. A. (2009). *Group performance.* Hove: Psychology Press.

OECD economic surveys India. (2007). Paris: OECD.

Peppers, D., & Rogers, M. (2010). *Managing customer relationships: A strategic framework.* Hoboken, NJ: John Wiley & Sons.

Perna, A., & Baraldi, E. (n.d.). *CRM systems in industrial companies: Intra- and inter-organizational effects.*

Robert-Ribes, J. (2012). *Connecting forward: Advanced networking for executives changing jobs, company, industry or country.* Leicester: Matador.

Samovar, L. A., Porter, R. E., & McDaniel, E. R. (2014). *Intercultural communication: A reader.* Boston: Cengage Learning.

Saxena, K. B., & Bharadwaj, S. S. (2007). *Business process outsourcing: For strategic advantage.* New Delhi: Excel Books.

Schroevers, S. (2013). *Where cultures meet; a cross-cultural comparison of business meeting styles.* Amsterdam.

Sharma, V., & Sharma, V. (2012). *Web-based and traditional outsourcing.* Boca Raton, FL: CRC Press.

Tho, L. I. (2004). *An investigation of the interaction between risk types in the outsourcing of the information technology function.*

Trent, R. J., & Roberts, L. R. (2010). *Managing global supply and risk: Best practices, concepts, and strategies.* Fort Lauderdale, FL: J. Ross Pub.

Trent, R. J., & Roberts, L. R. (2010). *Managing global supply and risk: Best practices, concepts, and strategies.* Fort Lauderdale, FL: J. Ross Pub.

Vagadia, B. (2007). *Outsourcing to India - a legal handbook.* Berlin: Springer.

Vance, C., & Paik, Y. (2006). *Managing a global workforce: Challenges and opportunities in international human resource management.* Armonk, NY: M.E. Sharpe.

Woog, M. (2009). *Change Management according to a CRM implementation.* GRIN Verlag.

Thesis references

Backman, P., Holmberg, M., & Tonnby, D. (2006). *Key factors for successful offshore outsourcing projects* (Unpublished master's thesis). Göteborg University.

Salim, M., & Jain, S. (n.d.). *CRM Marketing Mantra: Indian Perspective* (Unpublished master's thesis). NICE Management College, Roorkee Road, Meerut.

Websites references

Asian Countries Top List of Outsourcing Destinations. (n.d.). Retrieved January 12, 2016, from http://blogs.wsj.com/corporate-intelligence/2014/09/15/asian-countries-top-list-of-outsourcing-destinations/

Definition of communication in English:. (n.d.). Retrieved January 12, 2016, from www.oxforddictionaries.com/definition/english/communication

English or Hinglish - which will India choose? - BBC News. (n.d.). Retrieved January 12, 2016, from www.bbc.com/news/magazine-20500312

Rahman, M. (2012, May 15). Language exodus reshapes India's schools. Retrieved May 15, 2012, from http://www.theguardian.com/education/2012/may/15/india-schools-english

Appendices

Introduction: These interviews conducted at Helios Solutions will be the main support of my study. According to the topic, I have chosen the persons better positioned to provide relevant information for my practical study. No evidence has shown that the answers of my questions were reliable and true. However, I hope that my respondents gave honest answers to my investigation.

Language proficiency
(Interview with Akash Soni – Indian Websites Project manager)

1. How would you rate your English developers' skills?
2. English is the language used to interact between developers and international project managers. In which part of the project's process language proficiency plays the most important role?
3. In case of miscommunication during a project, what strategy do you implement?

Communication style and relationship building
(Interview with a developer – Name will not be disclosed)

1. What is your apprehension before working with any international colleague?
2. Is internal relationship building impact a project's outcome?
3. Is a good atmosphere at work motivates you to work more?

External communication in a cross-cultural environment
(Interview with Ashish Sharma – Business developer)

1. How would you define "external communication"? How important is to have an efficient external communication?
2. The international project manager is working only for 6 months. How can you for this reason maintain continuity with the client? What is your solution to ensure a smooth transition?

Technology knowledge

(Interview with Akash Soni – Indian Websites Project manager)

1. Could you give us your definition of "technology knowledge"?
2. How important is to have a qualified staff? Is quality always related to a high-skilled team?
3. Are there technologies (in development) you are not able to do? What to do in this case?
4. Do you have in mind that some technologies are used less and could in some time not be used anymore? Do you have any plan for that?

Creating a strategic partnership

(Interview with Jigar Shah – Helios Solutions' CEO)

1. Why do you work exclusively for the European market? Why not for the USA?
2. Are you thinking one day of hiring an internal project manager for long-term contract?
3. What are the motives that lead to succeed in outsourcing in India?
4. How a partnership can affect the team's performance and the project's outcome?
5. What are the next plans for Helios Solutions? Are you preparing the future?

YOUR KNOWLEDGE HAS VALUE